W0019846

THERE ARE MOMS WAY WORSE THAN YOU

Irrefutable Proof That You Are Indeed a Fantastic Parent

GLENN BOOZAN
Illustrated by Priscilla Witte

WORKMAN PUBLISHING • NEW YORK

Copyright © 2022 by Glenn Boozan

Hachette Book Group supports the right to free expression and the value of copyright. The purpose of copyright is to encourage writers and artists to produce the creative works that enrich our culture.

The scanning, uploading, and distribution of this book without permission is a theft of the author's intellectual property. If you would like permission to use material from the book (other than for review purposes), please contact permissions@hbgusa.com. Thank you for your support of the author's rights.

Workman
Workman Publishing
Hachette Book Group, Inc.
1290 Avenue of the Americas
New York, NY 10104
workman.com

Workman is an imprint of Workman Publishing, a division of Hachette Book Group, Inc. The Workman name and logo are registered trademarks of Hachette Book Group, Inc.

Design by Rae Ann Spitzenberger
Illustrations by Priscilla Witte

The publisher is not responsible for websites (or their content) that are not owned by the publisher.

Workman books may be purchased in bulk for business, educational, or promotional use. For information, please contact your local bookseller or the Hachette Book Group Special Markets Department at special.markets@hbgusa.com.

First Edition March 2022

Printed in China on responsibly sourced paper.

10 9 8 7 6 5 4 3 2 1

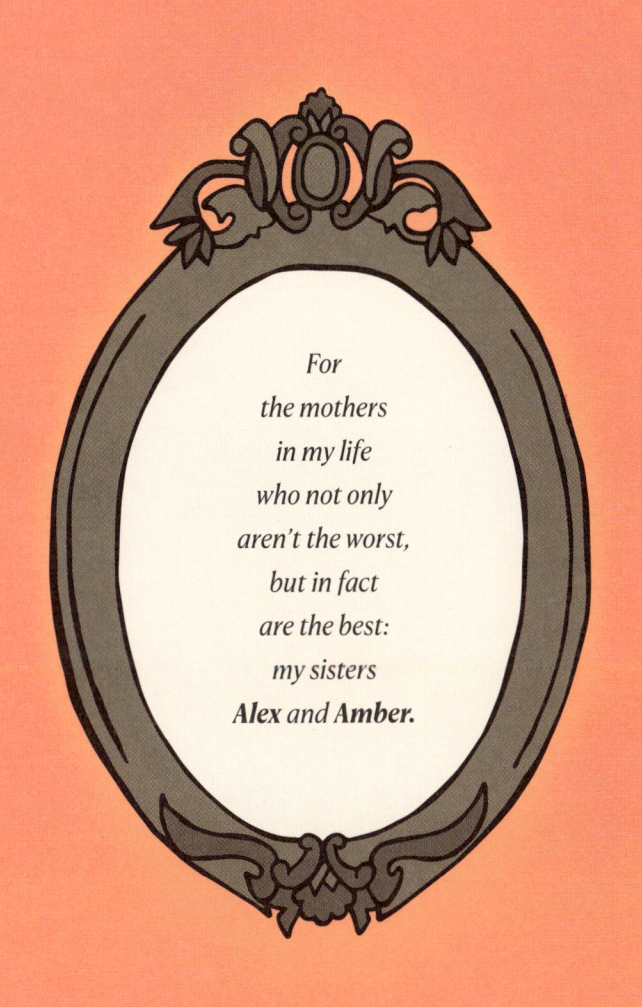

*For
the mothers
in my life
who not only
aren't the worst,
but in fact
are the best:
my sisters*
Alex *and* **Amber.**

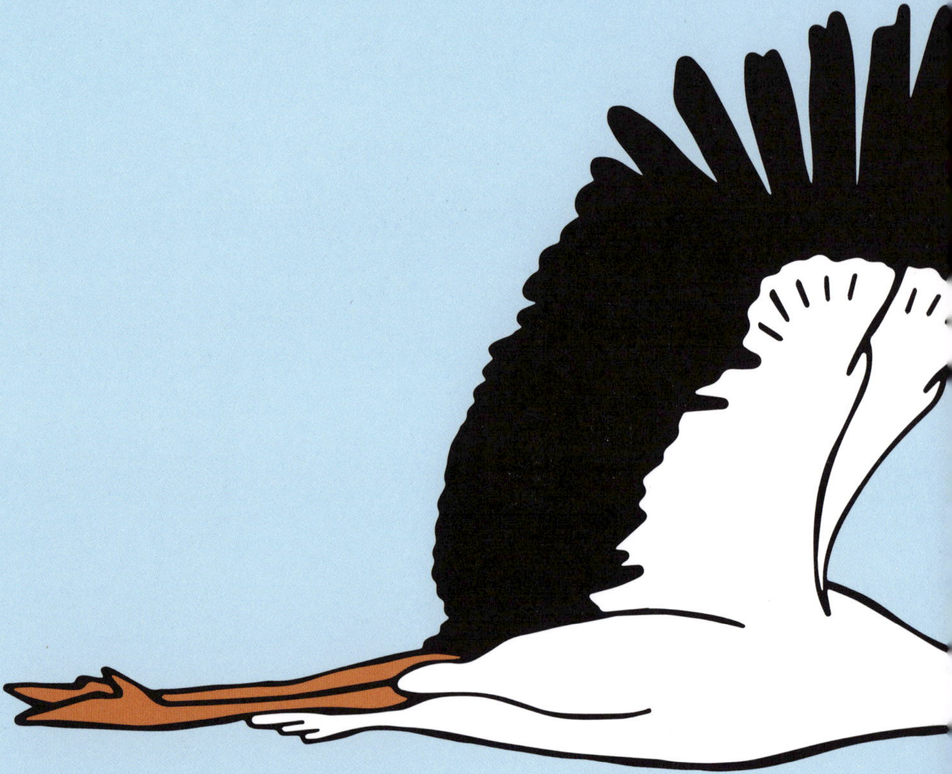

Congrats,
you had a kid (or two)!
Oh, what a time of joy.

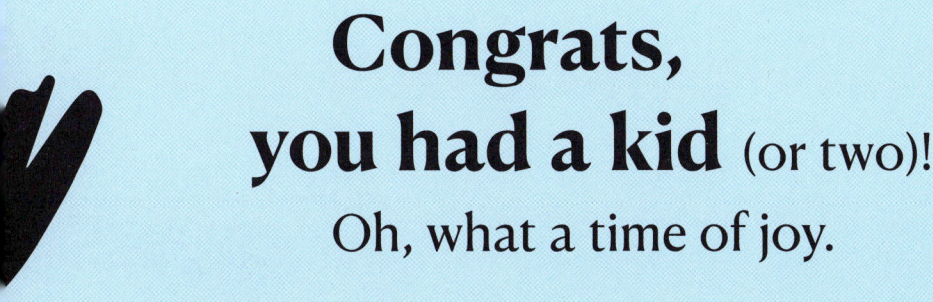

You got the crib,
 the car seat, bib;
you bought the perfect toys.

You read the books,
you did the work,
you **baby-proofed**
your stuff.

But even so,
a nagging thought:
**What if it's
not enough?**

Like...

"What if I don't burp them right?

Or what if I'm **too strict?**

Or what if I buy diapers, then the diapers make them sick?"

"Or what if they get **tetanus,**

or I don't dress them right?

Or what if when I strap them in, the Baby Björn's **too tight??"**

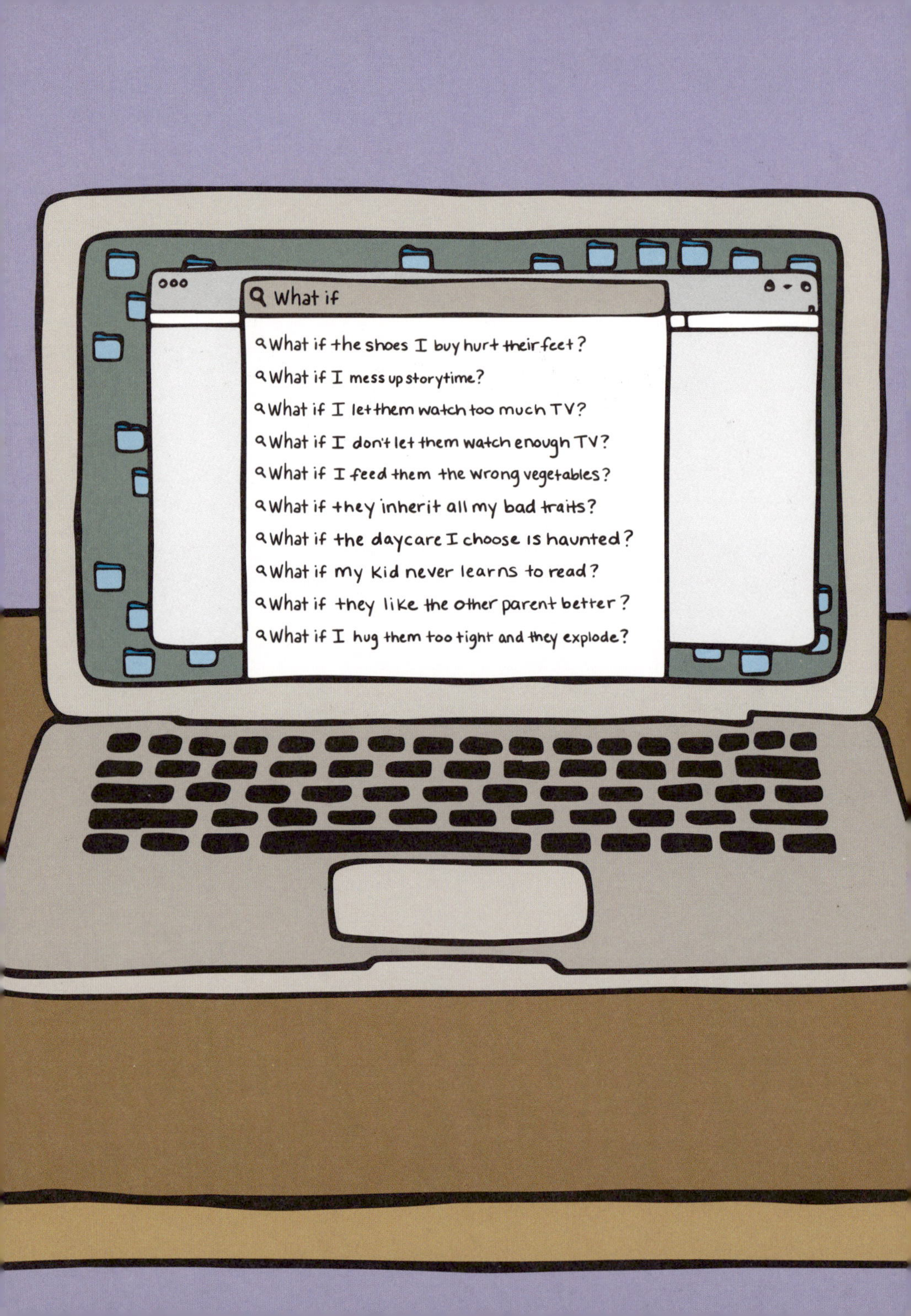
What if
What if the shoes I buy hurt their feet?
What if I mess up storytime?
What if I let them watch too much TV?
What if I don't let them watch enough TV?
What if I feed them the wrong vegetables?
What if they inherit all my bad traits?
What if the daycare I choose is haunted?
What if my kid never learns to read?
What if they like the other parent better?
What if I hug them too tight and they explode?

"Or maybe," your head starts to spin, it's now a **full-blown panic,**

"They lose an eye, or even worse, their food is not organic?

"Or what if I'm not watching and they stumble off a cliff?

"Or if I pick the wrong preschool? **What if, what if, what if—?"**

⚠ Warning

SYSTEM OVERLOAD

- What if my kid never learns to read?
- What if they like the other parent better?
- What if I hug them too tight and they explode?

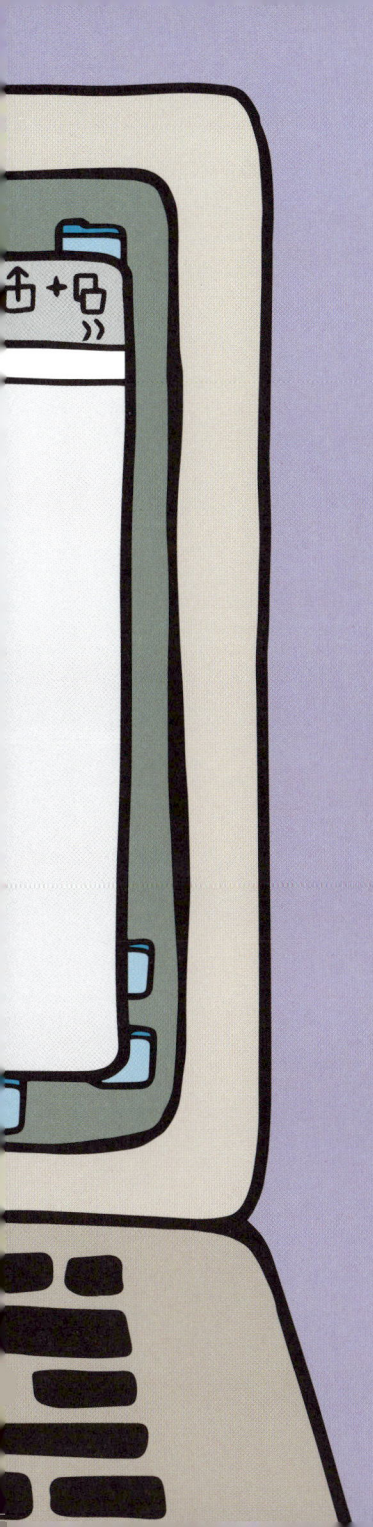

WHOA,
okay, calm down.
Take a deep breath,
big exhale.

It's absolutely normal,
feeling like you're
doomed to fail.

And though you'll make some
big mistakes,
remember this is true:

When put into perspective, there are moms **WAY** worse than you.

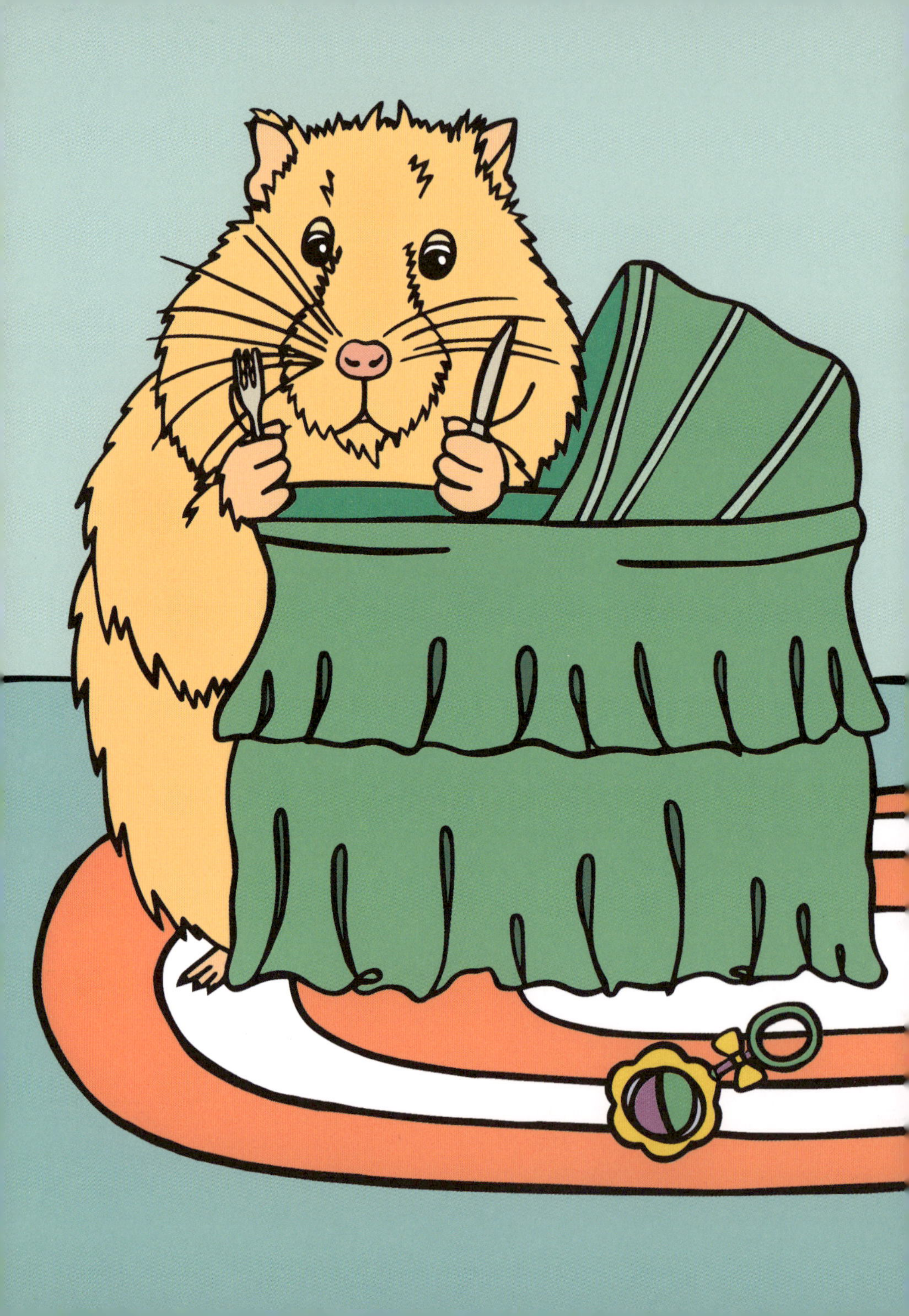

You won't be worse than
hamster moms,
no matter how you try.

Sometimes they eat
their **newborn pups.**
We still don't yet know why.

A **mom giraffe** is pretty nice until the fetus drops:

She'll birth a newborn baby calf, then **kick him 'til he walks.**

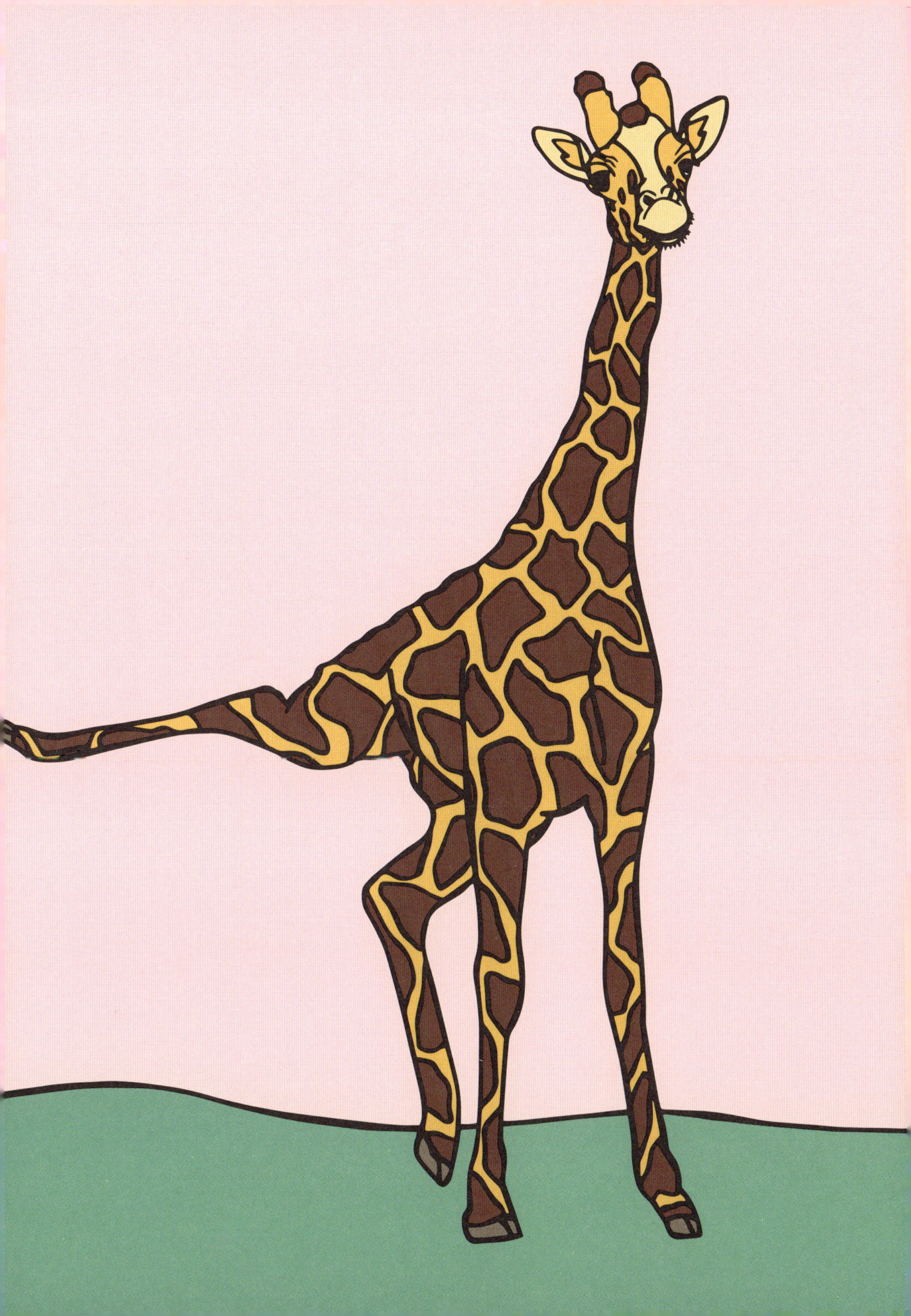

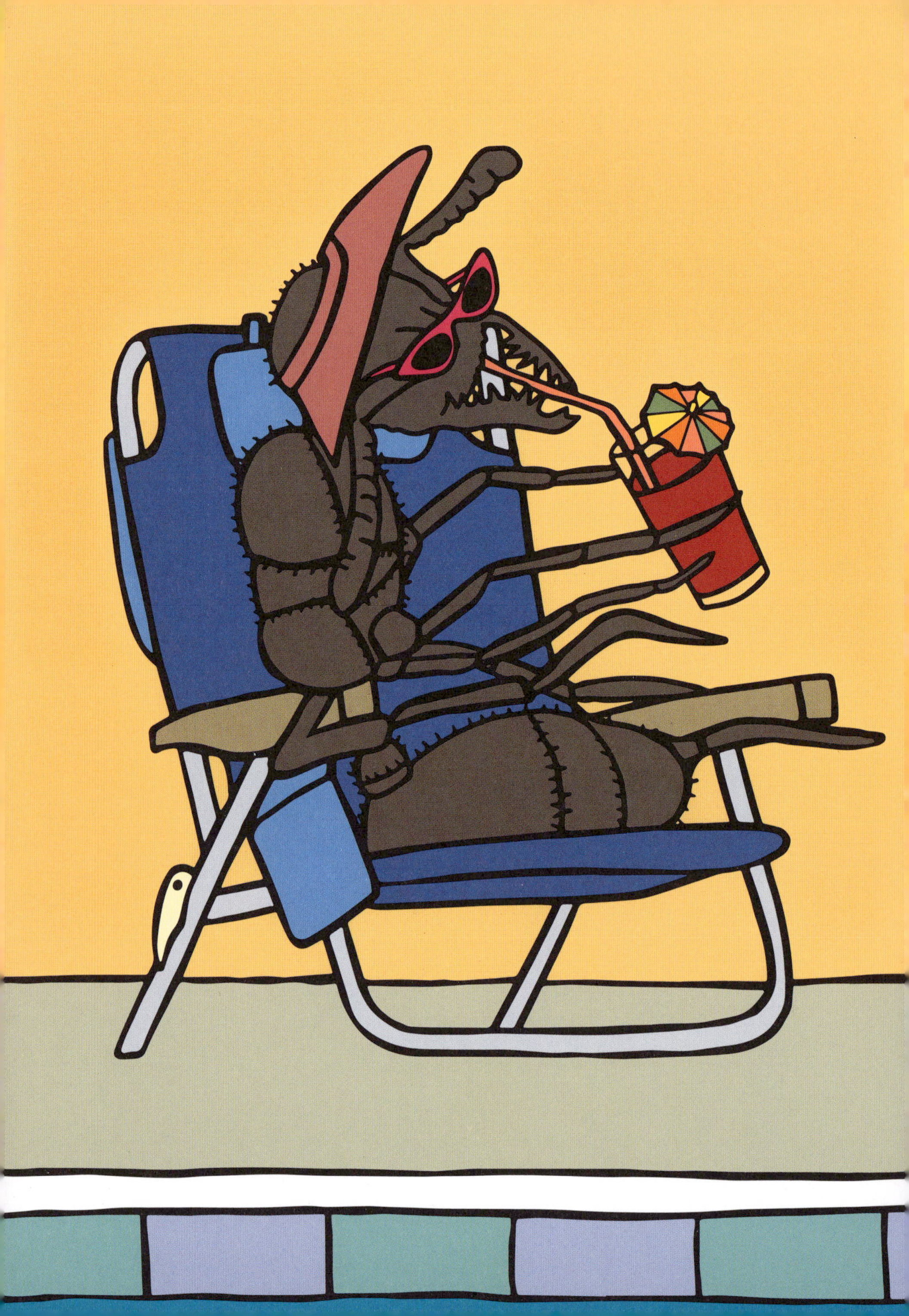

If someone calls you
"selfish mom"
and makes you feel like crud,

Tell them sometimes
Dracula ants
will suck their babies' blood.

Whenever you feel **guilty** that you haven't cleaned the house:

Sexton beetles
raise their kids
in a **decomposing mouse.**

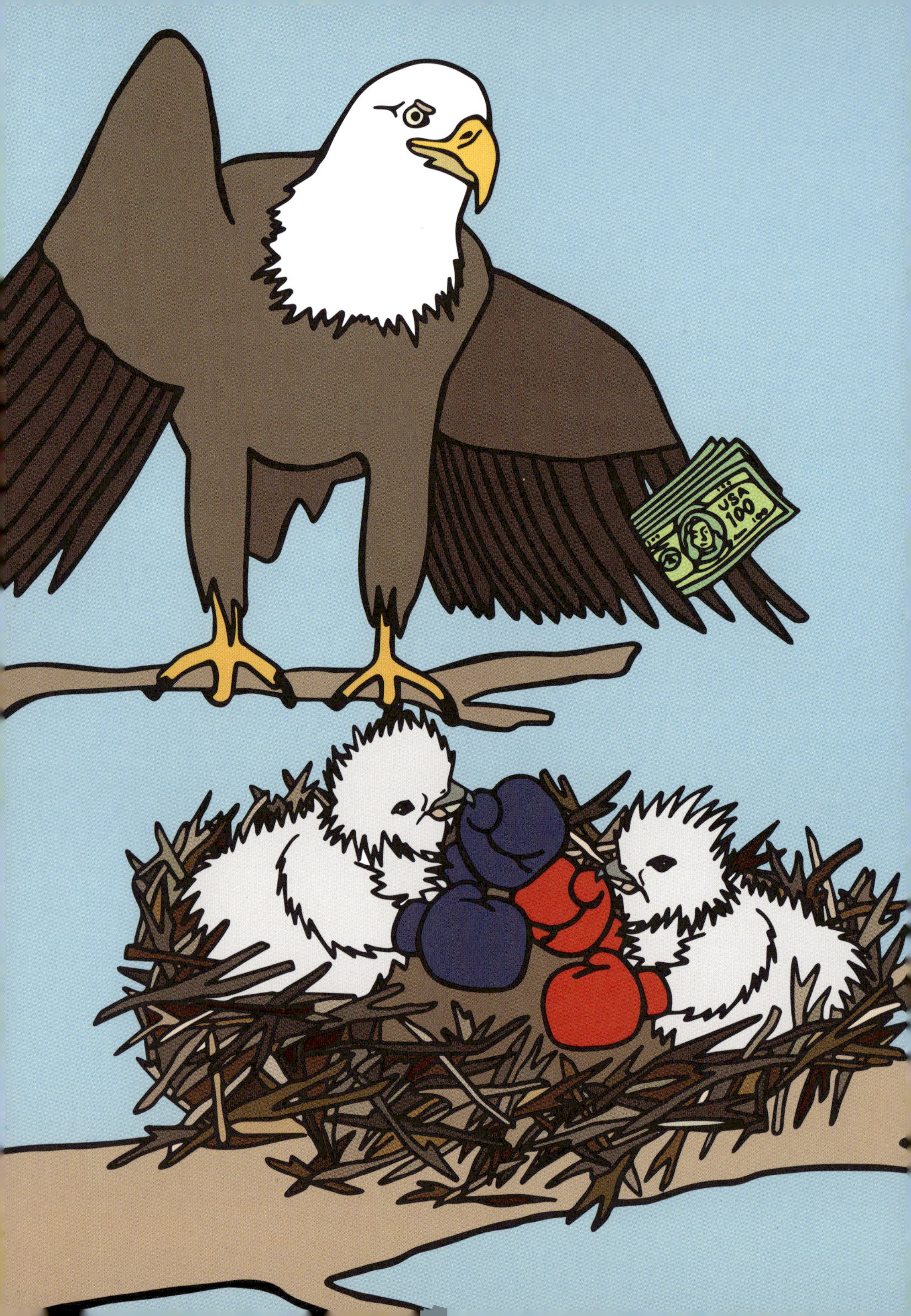
USA
100

An **eagle mom** believes
in survival of the strong.

She'll let her little eaglets fight
until the death (how wrong).

Panda moms
are perfect,
unless they're blessed
with two.

Twins are hard,
so they'll **ditch one**—
it's terrible. And true!

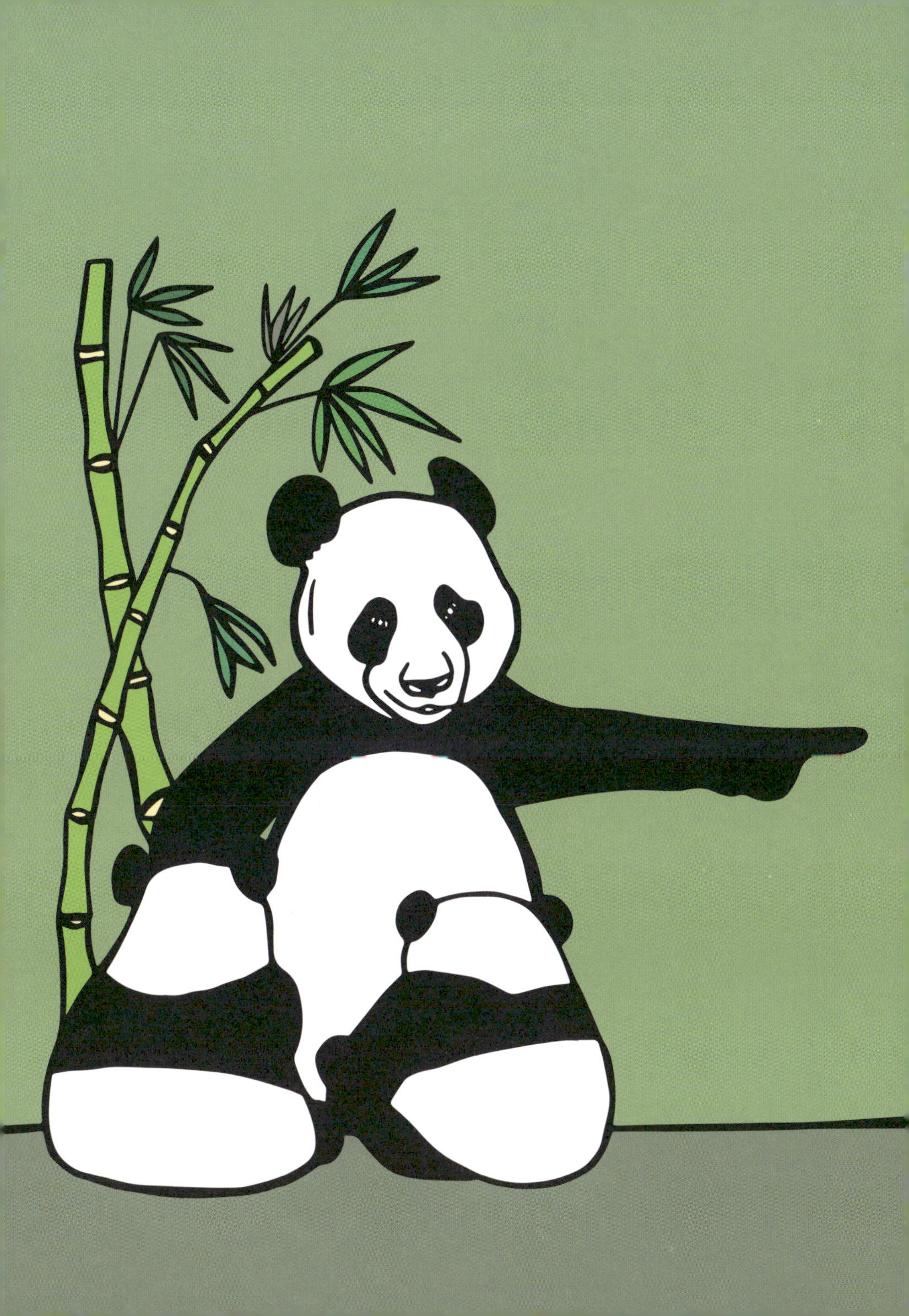

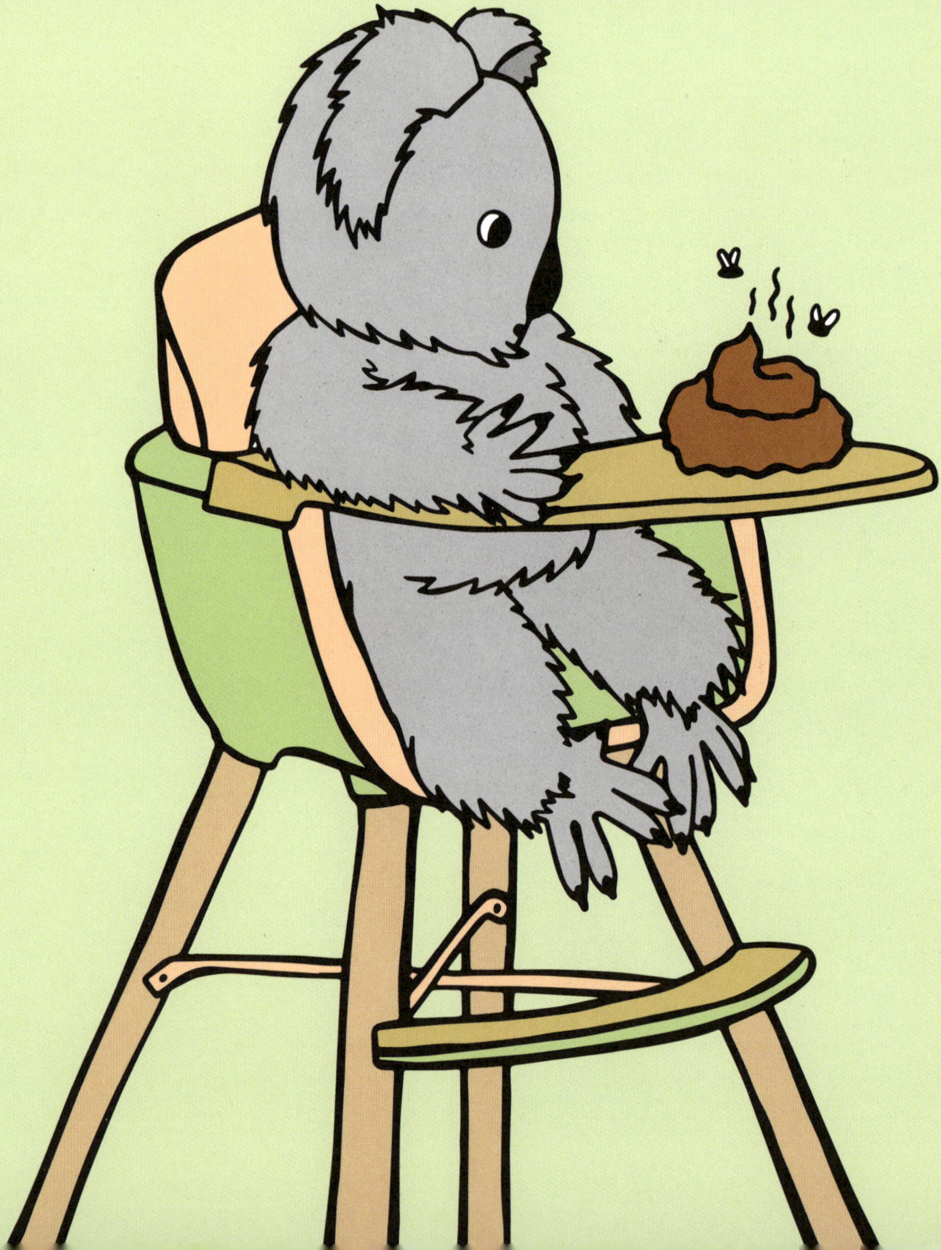

For dinnertime, a **koala mom** will feed her kids her poop.

Remember that when you feel bad for giving yours **fast food.**

When side by side **with Lanyu skinks,** you'd look like World's Best Mama.

They'll **eat their eggs**
 if things get tough,
  just to avoid the drama.

If a quokka mom
comes face to face
with dingoes in the wild,

Guess what she'll do
to get away?
That's right—she'll
toss her child.

At least you're not a
cuckoo mom.
Whoo boy, that bitch
is brazen.

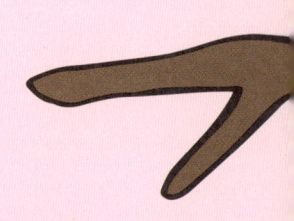

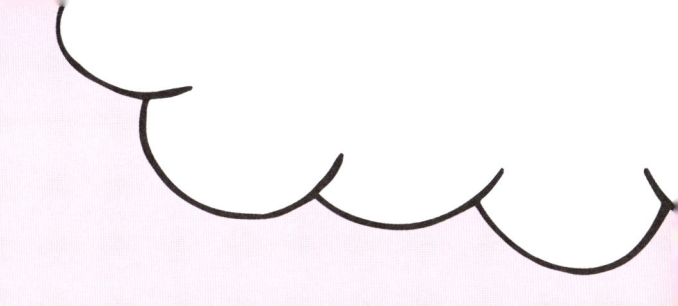

She **hides her eggs**

in other nests so she won't have to raise 'em.

NOT A CUCKOO EGG

Harp seals? Oh, they're super cute. Maternally? They're frightening.

Two weeks
 after giving birth,
 they're **outta there**
 like lightning.

In fact, a lot of new moms pull a **disappearing act:**

Bunnies, black bears, snakes and lizards, sheep and birds and cats.

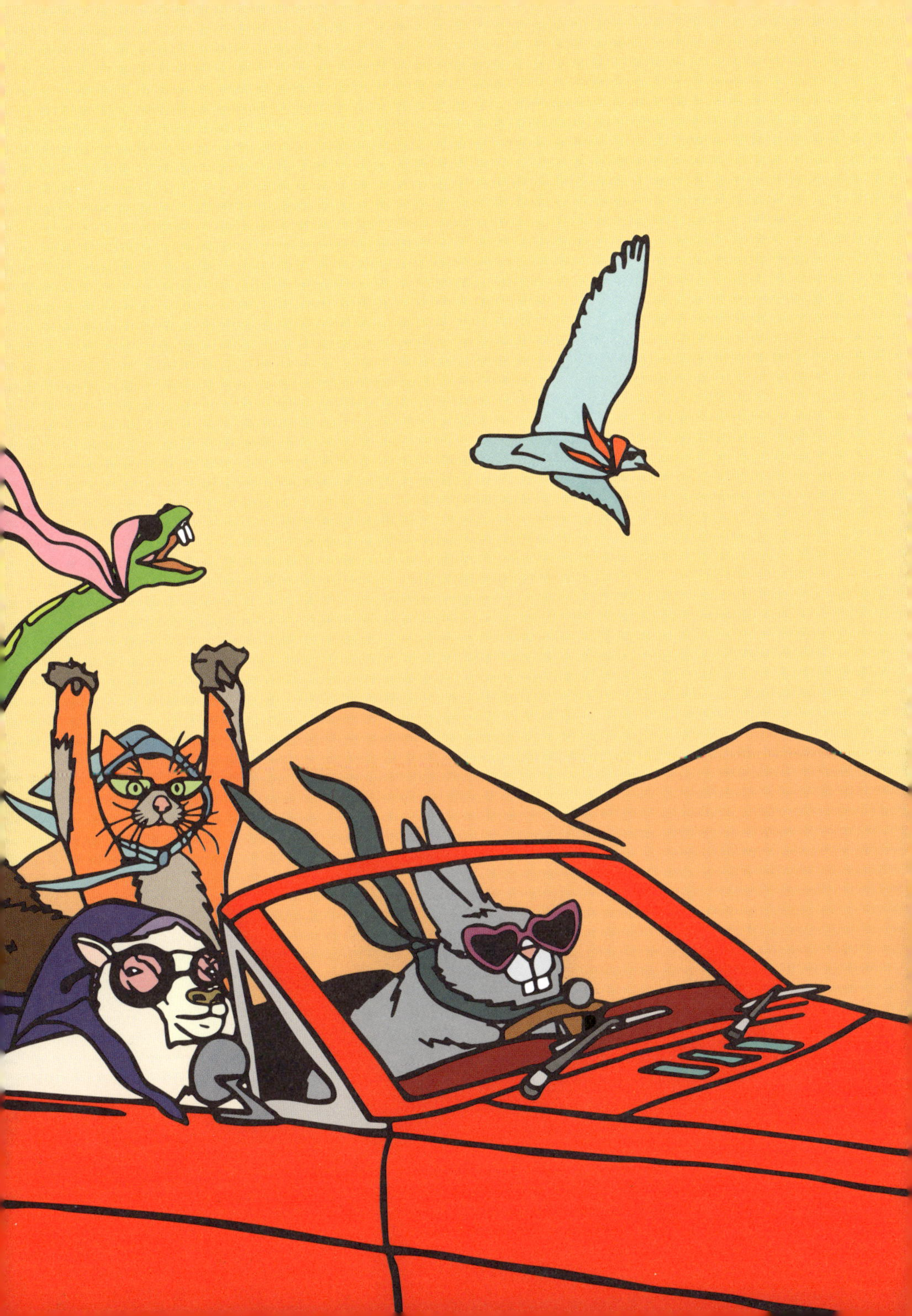

Alaskan plovers,
they don't even fake it
like they care.

One month
 after giving birth?
First class, **Hawaiian Air.**

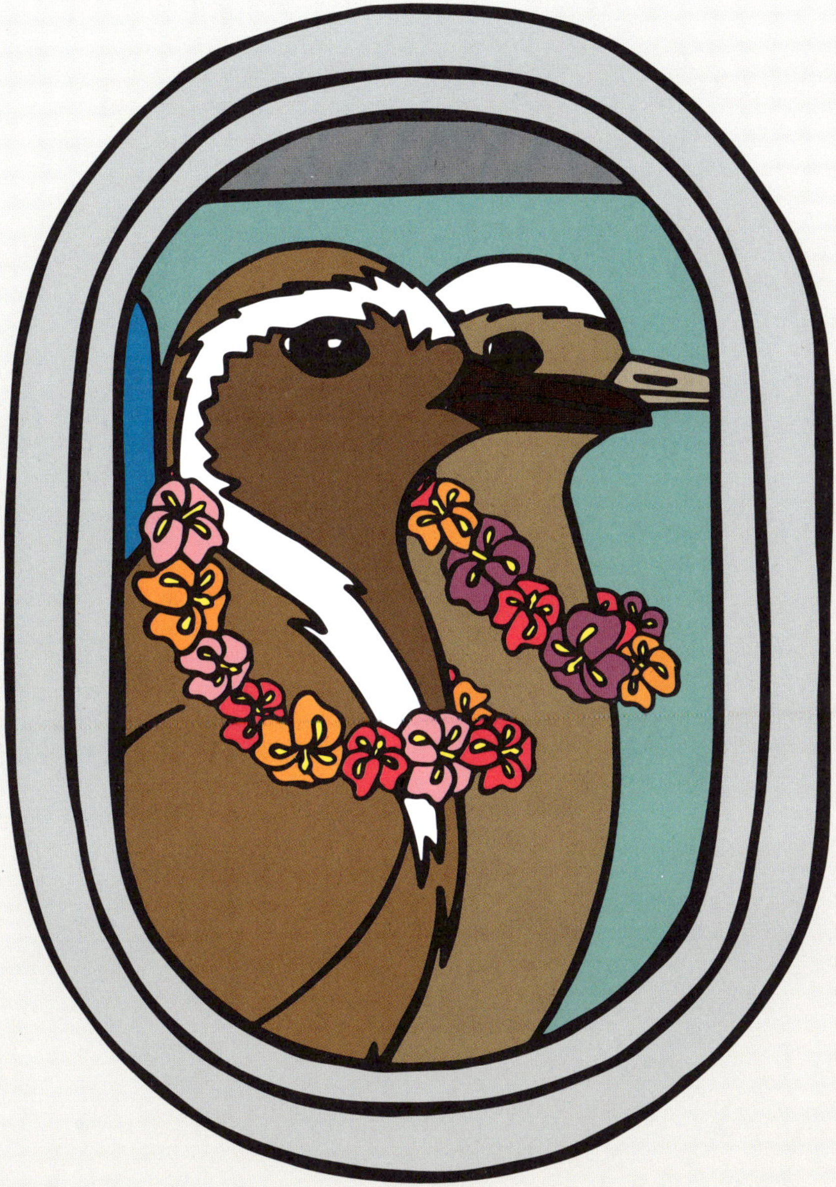

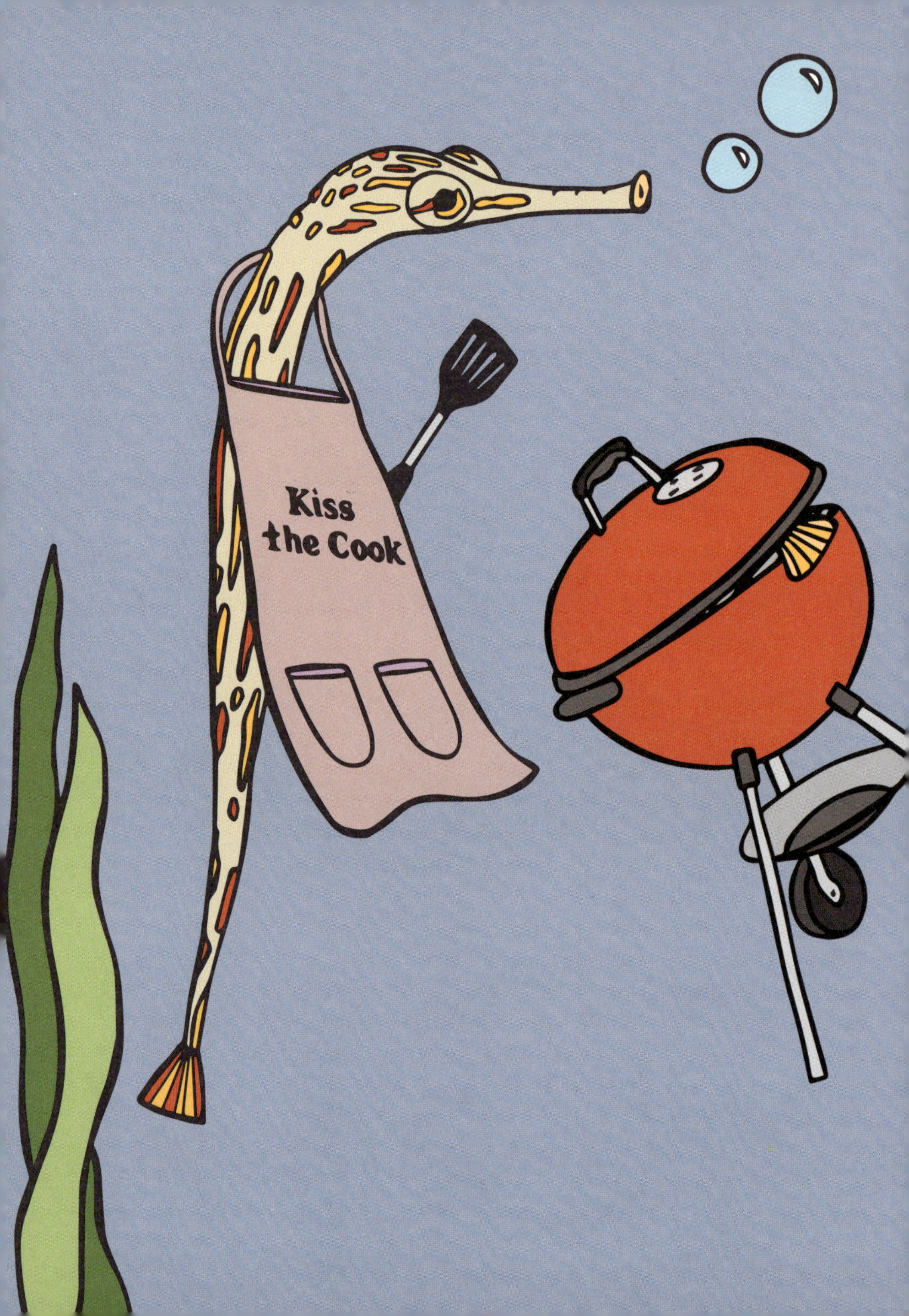
Kiss
the Cook

It's not just moms,
some **dads suck too!**
They're not all warm
and snuggly.

A pipefish dad
will eat his kids
if he thinks that
they're ugly.

Horses seem like super dads, but, eh, they're not the best.

They'll threaten
other horses' kids
and kick them
**straight
to death.**

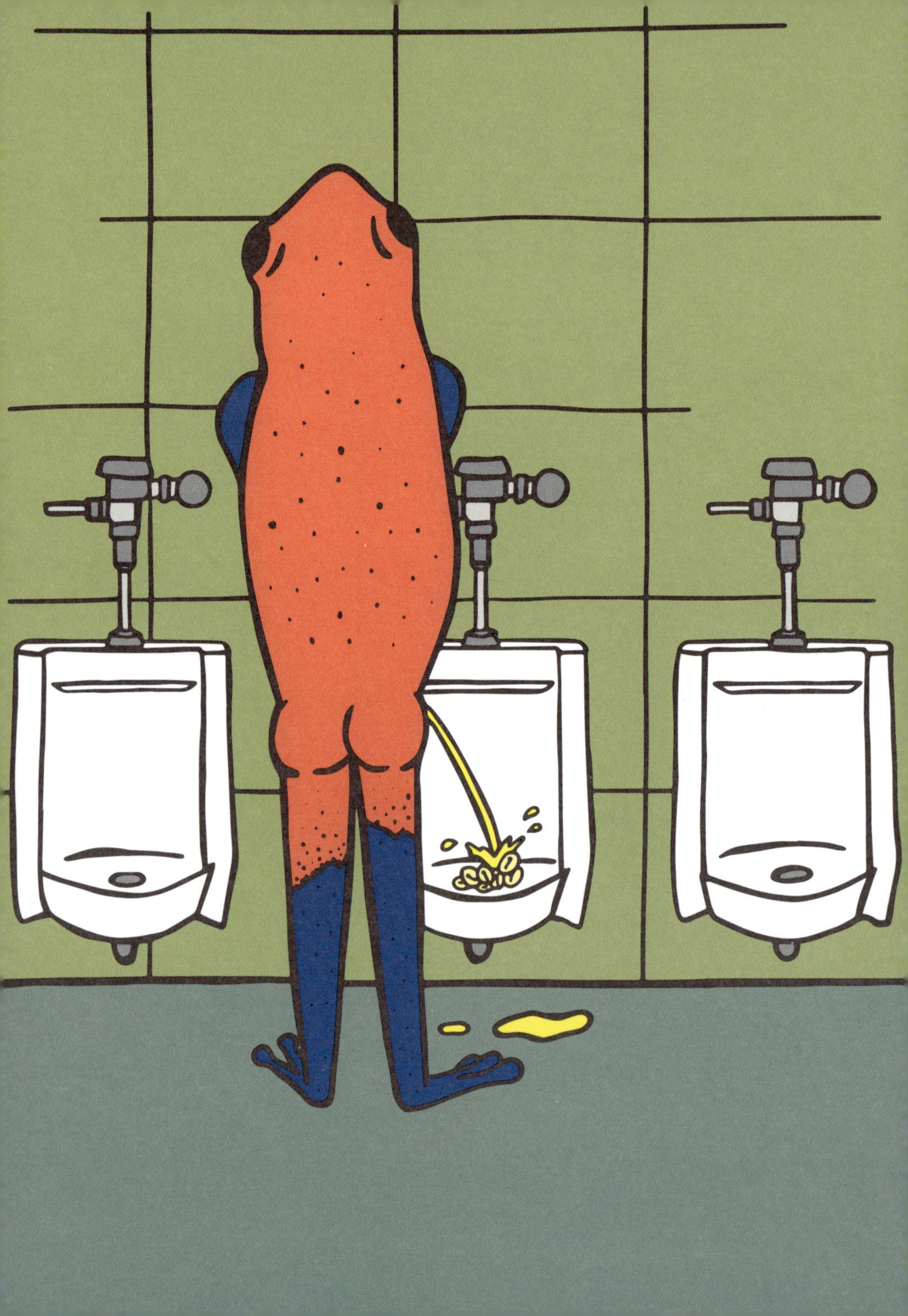

The **poison dart frog** dad
is less a "hit"
and more a "miss."

To keep his eggs
from drying out,
he'll sometimes
use his piss.

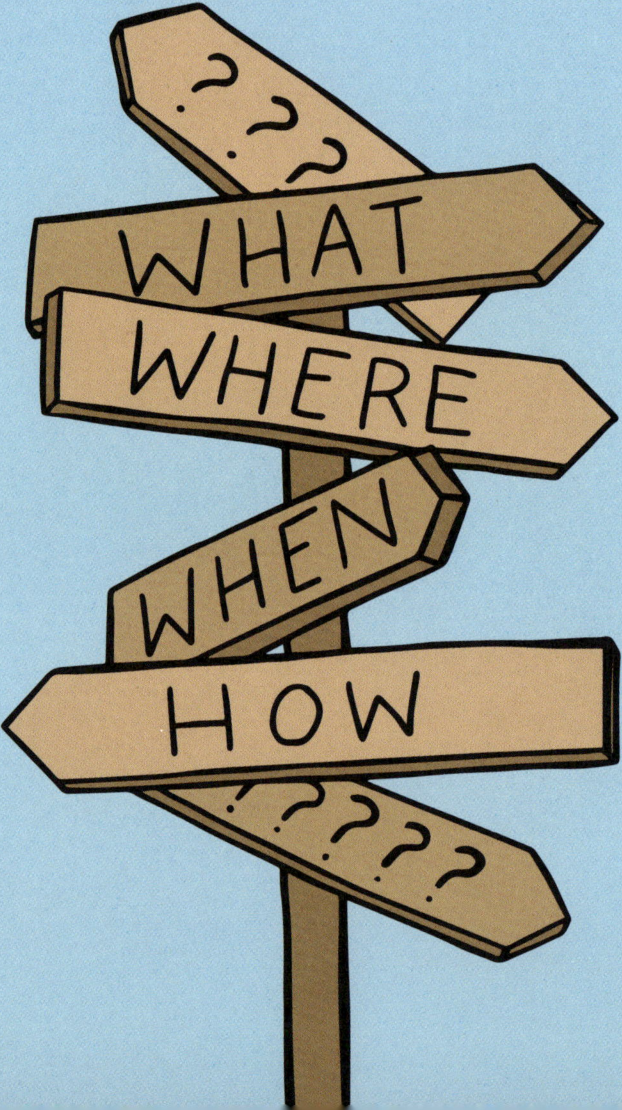
???
WHAT
WHERE
WHEN
HOW
????

So when you feel
    exhausted, or there's
too much on your plate,

    As long as you
        don't eat your baby?
Yeah, **you're doing great.**

Raising kids is chaos;
    there is no ideal path.

Like anything worth doing,
    motherhood will
kick your ass.

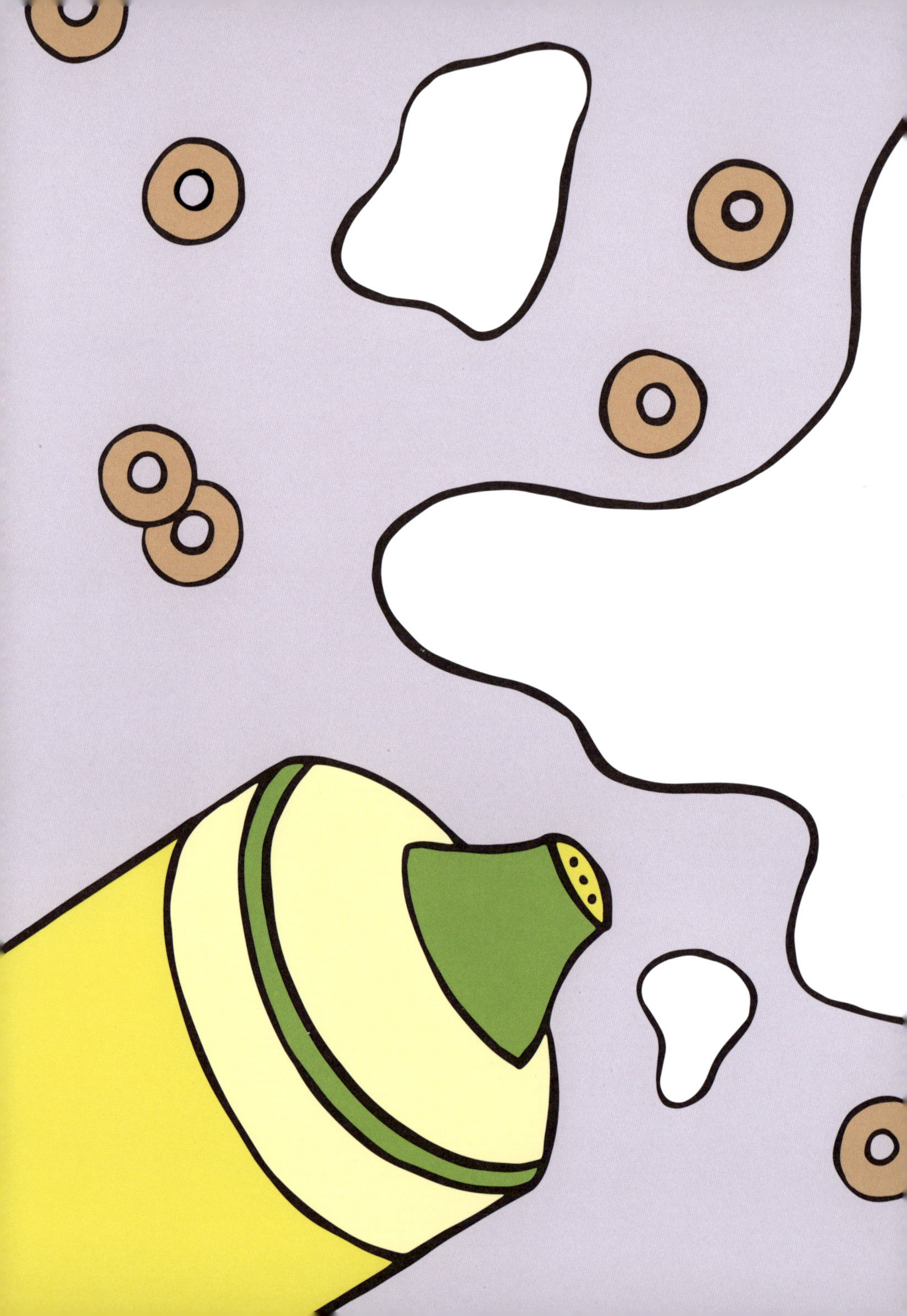

When the **panic** rises,
and the **pressure**
starts to mount,

Remember that
you're trying...
and *that* is all
that counts.

Though others might
    make comments, or judge
from where they sit,

This concept of a
"perfect mom"
is absolute bullshit.

Let's celebrate the
not-so-great and
"Wish it had gone better!"

Embrace the mediocre family
    times you share together.

PARTICIPATION AWARD
BEST MOM
CERTIFICA
OF
MEDIOCRITY
Diploma
OK-est Mom of the YEAR
#5

'Cause even if you
drop a kid,
or "accidentally" curse,

Just know that
when it comes
to moms...

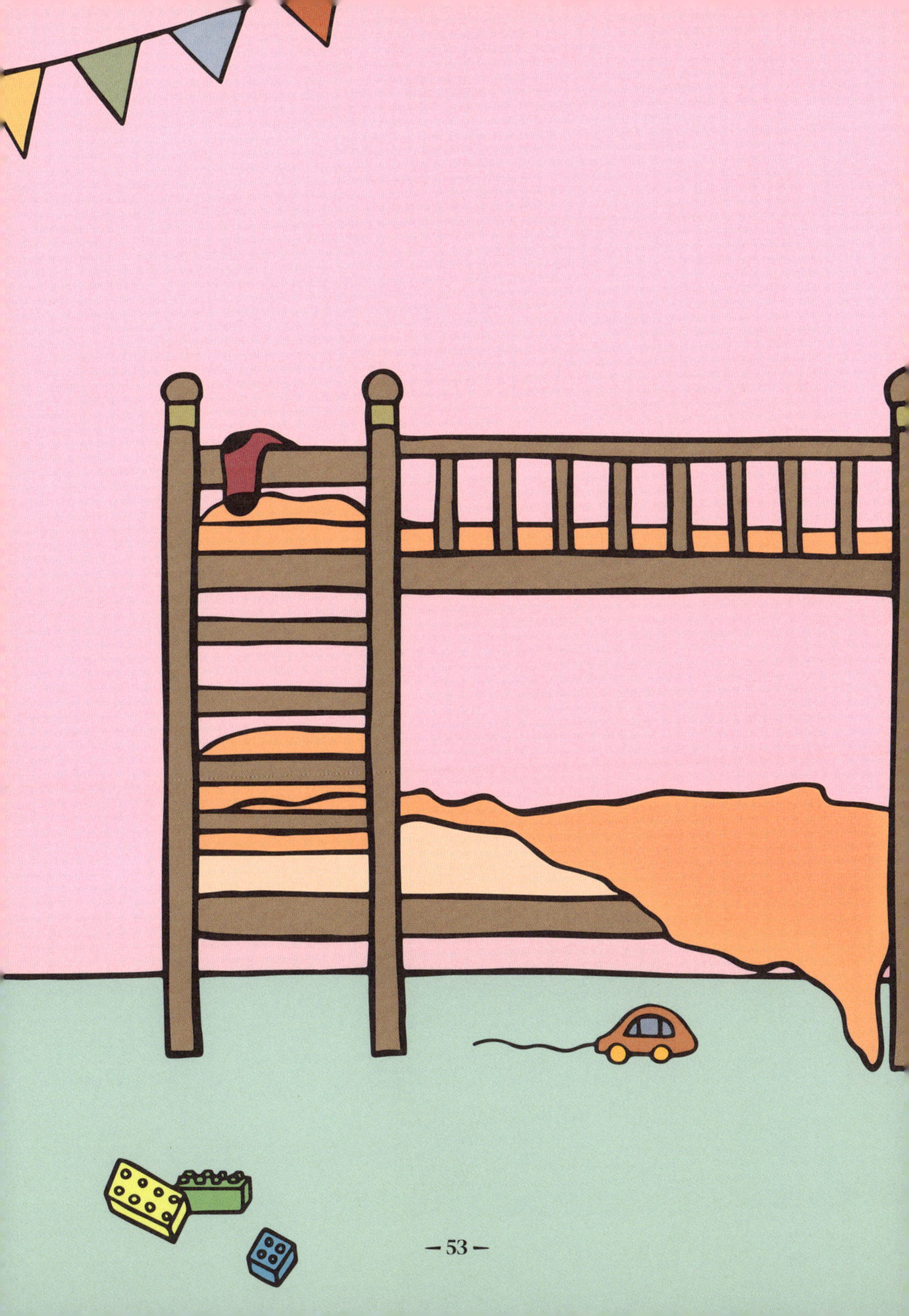

… you'll never be the worst!

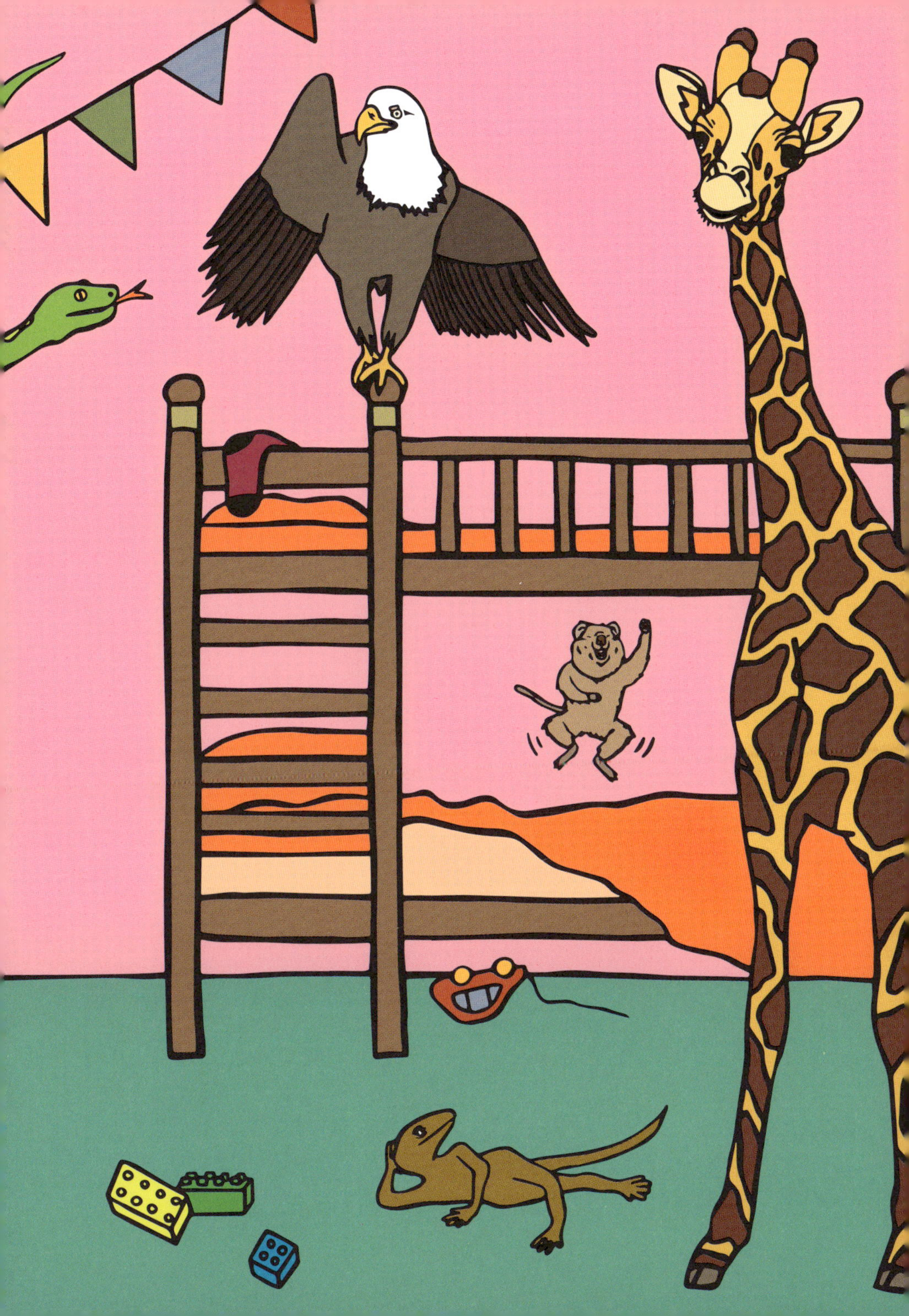

APPENDIX

Though these may appear to be nature's most truly heinous animal moms and dads, a more in-depth look reveals that just like the rest of us, these parents are doing the very best they can.

Hamsters

Perhaps the most infamous bad moms of the animal kingdom, hamster mothers have been known to eat their pups shortly after giving birth. Experts still don't know *exactly* why they behave cannibalistically, but at least one study points to a vitamin B deficiency brought on by a heavy diet of corn. Other theories point to stress, lack of food, size of litter, or, if the babies have been handled, an unfamiliar scent that may confuse the hamster mom from recognizing the babies as her own.

Giraffes

Because giraffes give birth standing up, a baby giraffe begins its life with an 8-foot freefall to Earth. It learns to stand about 30 minutes later, and walks a short time after that. If the mother feels that the baby is progressing too slowly, she'll provide "encouragement" to her newborn by kicking its legs until it can walk on its own. As with many parents in the animal kingdom, the giraffe's behavior is about survival: About half of baby giraffes get eaten by predators, so their mom's protective instincts seem warranted.

Dracula ants

Dracula ant queens don't have the excuse of cannibalizing their young for lack of available food. In bigger colonies, *even if there's other food available*, the queen feeds exclusively on the blood (or hemolymph) of her own larvae. She chooses a victim, usually in the final stages of development (and therefore most nutrient-rich), then stabs it with her jaw and drinks its blood like a horrifying little milkshake. Though this process doesn't kill the larvae, it does leave visible puncture wounds. Scientists believe this type of feeding is preferable because it's more energy efficient: The predigested nutrients in the larvae's blood are easier to absorb than normal food.

Sexton beetles

The Sexton beetle, aka the burying beetle, really does raise its young inside a carcass. It uses specialized antennae to sniff out the body of a small dead animal, usually a mouse or a bird. Before burying the animal to protect it from predators, the beetles clean the carcass, then coat it with oral and anal secretions (yes, you read that right) to prevent decay. The female lays her eggs in the ground, then once they've hatched, they all move into the carcass itself. If the carcass is too small to fit all the hatchlings, the mom will kill a few baby beetles to make room.

Eagles

Eagle moms really do allow their eaglets to engage in what is known as siblicide, though it may not be as common as is sometimes reported. When it does happen, the first chick in the nest to hatch (being larger and hungrier) is usually the aggressor. It challenges its younger sibling (most eagles lay two eggs) by driving it to the edge of the nest so the two won't have to share attention and resources. Some studies cite parental neglect as a cause of eagle siblicide, noting that it may be avoided if the mom brings back enough food for both eaglets.

Pandas

Pandas aren't great at becoming parents in the first place. Unfortunately for female pandas, once they finally do become mothers, panda dads are absent, rarely even meeting their offspring. Even with only one child to care for, panda moms have been known to undernourish their babies (panda moms often don't get enough nutrients from bamboo, and therefore don't produce enough milk) or accidentally crush their cubs while nursing. With twins, the mother panda may simply become overwhelmed and eventually abandon the weaker twin. But even in captive environments with a full team of zoologists, the weaker panda cub sometimes doesn't survive.

Koalas

Like most marsupials, koala cubs start off drinking their mom's milk. Then after about six months, the babies instinctively nuzzle their heads down toward their mother's rear end to eat her poop. The reason? Fresh eucalyptus leaves are too toxic for a baby koala's stomach, and not only does the mom's digestive process neutralize those toxins, but the poop also contains helpful nutrients. (The next time you feel guilty about letting your kids eat cold pizza for breakfast, it's worth remembering that a koala's first solid meal is its mother's feces.)

Lanyu skinks

Parental care in the reptile world is rare, so the long-tailed Lanyu Island skink's practice of filial cannibalism (eating one's young) is not entirely surprising. But it *is* different: Most lizards abandon the nest shortly after laying a clutch of eggs; however, the Lanyu skink lays its eggs and sticks around to ward off potential predators . . . until she feels the danger is too great. If a snake threatens her nest one too many times, she'll consume her eggs rather than sacrifice them to the intruding snake. Scientists hypothesize that Lanyu Island skinks eat the eggs to nourish and strengthen themselves while depriving the snake of a meal, too.

Quokkas

Okay, okay . . . quokka moms do not actually "throw" their babies. But they don't hold on to them either. When a quokka mom is carrying a newborn in her marsupial pouch and finds herself being chased by a predator, she creates a diversion as part of her escape plan: She will eject her joey by relaxing her pouch muscles, allowing it to fall to the ground. The joey serves as a yummy distraction for the predator while the mom runs to safety, hopefully to breed again.

Cuckoos

A European common cuckoo is known as a "brood parasite," or a type of animal that tricks others into raising its young for them. A cuckoo mom finds another bird's nest, surreptitiously deposits her egg inside, then flies miles away from the scene of the crime. The unsuspecting bird mom accepts and raises this strange new egg as her own. After the baby cuckoo hatches, it may even kill the nest's *original* baby birds to ensure it gets maximum resources. The cuckoo egg is often thicker shelled (cuckoos sometimes drop their eggs on existing host eggs to break one or more of them) and darker in color so that it blends into the shadows of the nest.

Harp seals

Harp seals are seemingly dedicated moms at first. They feed and dote on their newborn pups for twelve days before they disappear to go mate again, leaving the vulnerable babies sitting out in the open on a block of ice, unable to feed themselves. The pups then spend the next several weeks starving, losing about half their weight. Eventually, they learn to swim and hunt for themselves, but only 70 percent of them survive their first year of life (hey, at least they'll have something to talk about in therapy).

Plovers

During mating season, female plovers in Western Alaska will lay four eggs, which hatch about a month later. As soon as the eggs have hatched, both bird parents abandon their babies to make the 3,000-mile, 50-hour trip to Hawaii (one of the longest nonstop migrations of all birds). The hatchlings are left to figure life out on their own.

Pipefish

A pipefish is related to a seahorse, except without the "good dad" reputation. A pipefish father assumes the brunt of the pregnancy, carrying the eggs in his body until they're ready to be released. To separate the weak from the strong, he restricts nutrients to his pouch, allowing the heartier eggs to get all the food. Then he absorbs the remaining (weaker) eggs. The amount of eggs he "eats" varies, but if the female he mated with is perceived as weak or "unattractive," that pipefish dad will absorb more of her eggs than others'.

Horses

Stallions are beautiful, but it's true that they also sometimes murder other horses' children—particularly male foals. A number of other animals (including zebras, lions, squirrels, and sea lions) do, too, so it's not uncommon in the animal kingdom. Scientists reason that this happens because of competition for resources (like food and future mates). In rare instances, if a stallion suspects one of his mares has been impregnated by another—even if the horse isn't *totally* sure—he'll attack and try to kill the offspring. Scientifically speaking, he doesn't want to waste time and energy caring for another dude's foal.

Strawberry poison dart frogs

Frogs typically don't make the best parents, so it's a miracle the strawberry poison dart frog puts in any effort at all. After the tiny mom frog lays her batch of eggs on a leaf near the rain forest floor, it's the dad's turn to protect them by making sure they don't dry out or get eaten by predators. To keep the eggs moist, male poison dart frogs will transport water via its cloaca (a sort of reptilian anus/urethra combo) for about ten days until they hatch into tadpoles.